# Greater Than a T[
# Jacksonville
# Florida
# USA

## 50 Travel Tips from a Local

Jessica Ann French

Lock Haven, PA
All rights reserved.
ISBN: 9781549940583

# > TOURIST

Jessica French

# BOOK DESCRIPTION

Are you excited about planning your next trip?

Do you want to try something new?

Would you like some guidance from a local?

If you answered yes to any of these questions, then this Greater Than a Tourist book is for you.

Greater Than a Tourist by Jessica French offers the inside scoop on Jacksonville, Florida. Most travel books tell you how to sightsee. Although there's nothing wrong with that, as a part of the Greater than a Tourist series, this book will give you tips from someone who lives at your next travel destination. In these pages, you'll discover local advice that will help you throughout your trip.

Travel like a local. Slow down and get to know the people and the culture of a place. By the time you finish this book, you will be eager and prepared to travel to your next destination.

Jessica French

# TABLE OF CONTENTS

30. Cultural Activities: The PLAYERS Championship

31. Cultural Activities: Jacksonville Jazz Fest

32. Cultural Activities: Florida-Georgia

33. Cultural Activities: Gate River Run

34. Cultural Activities: One Spark

35. Cultural Activities: 4th of July Fireworks

36. Cultural Activities: Brew at the Zoo

37. Sports

38. Sports- The Jacksonville Jaguars

39. Sports- The Jacksonville Jumbo Shrimp

41. Notable Places- Florida Theater

42. Notable Places- The Jacksonville Landing

43. Notable Places- St. Augustine Amphitheatre

44. Notable Places- Jacksonville Zoo & Gardens

45. Nature

46. Nature- Guana National Wildlife Preserve

47. Nature- Amelia Island State Park

48. Nature- Fort Clinch State Park

49. Nature- Anastasia State Park

50. The Legend- Shahid Khan

**Jessica French**

Top Reasons to Book This Trip

Our Story

# DEDICATION

This book is dedicated to my travel companion, best friend, and husband, Damien Zouaoui.

Jessica French

# ABOUT THE AUTHOR

Jessica French graduated with a BS in Psychology from Florida State University in May of 2013. Immediately after graduating, Jessica moved to Jacksonville, Florida where she enjoyed the diversity of the city during her three years of working and living there.

After moving to New York City and continuing to climb the corporate ladder, Jessica decided to follow her heart and leave her stable job behind to follow a more unconventional lifestyle. Jessica is now living life on the road as a digital nomad on an indefinite round-the-world adventure.

Jessica French

# HOW TO USE THIS BOOK

The Greater Than a Tourist book series was written by someone who has lived in an area for over three months. The goal of this book is to help travelers either dream or experience different locations by providing opinions from a local. The author has made suggestions based on their own experiences. Please do your own research before traveling to the area in case the suggested places are unavailable.

Jessica French

# FROM THE PUBLISHER

Traveling can be one of the most important parts of a person's life. The anticipation and memories that you have are some of the best. As a publisher of the Greater Than a Tourist book series, as well as the popular 50 Things to Know book series, we strive to help you learn about new places, spark your imagination, and inspire you. Wherever you are and whatever you do I wish you safe, fun, and inspiring travel.

Lisa Rusczyk Ed. D.

CZYK Publishing

Jessica French

# WELCOME TO > TOURIST

Jessica French

# INTRODUCTION

Not many people know that Jacksonville, Florida is the largest city by area in the continental United States, boasting over 840 square miles of beaches, suburban neighborhoods, business centers, and natural preserves. Jacksonville is also home to the St. Johns River, one of the only two rivers in the United States that flows north instead of south.

With its large land mass, it's not surprising that Jacksonville has a diverse range of landscapes and cultural areas, each with its own vibe and history. From sleepy beach towns to vibrant downtown business communities, Jacksonville has a little piece of everything.

Jessica French

# 1. Best Times to Visit

The beautiful thing about Florida is that any time of year is the perfect time to visit. No matter if it is the middle of July or late December, you can still find people riding their bikes around town or soaking up the sun at the beach.

If we had to pick one season though, summer is the most ideal time to visit, as there are many activities and festivals going on around town. For those coming from up north though, summer might feel a little too hot and humid for your enjoyment, so it might be more ideal to come in the early spring.

## 2. How to Get to Jacksonville

Jacksonville is located on what's called "The First Coast". Only a few miles from Georgia, Jacksonville is right at the intersection of I-10 and I-95, making it an easy drive from many places in America. Jacksonville has an international airport as well, but flights are often 2 – 3x more expensive than flying into Savannah, Georgia or Orlando, Florida. So if you don't mind making a stop somewhere before coming to Jacksonville, consider flying into Savannah or Orlando, and then rent a car for the short two hour drive to Jax.

## 3.  What to Pack

When packing for Jacksonville, consider bringing what you would pack for any type of beach vacation. This means bathing suits, hats, sunscreen, and dresses. The local Jacksonville style is extremely casual, so even if you are going out to a nice dinner or to one of the few dance clubs, don't expect to see people dressed to the nines like you would in LA or Manhattan.

During the summer, the typical garb for ladies is a sun dress and sandals. Or when it gets a little chilly at night in the winter, you can find locals wearing jeans, boots, and a sweater.

Not sure if it's a good thing or a bad thing, but Jacksonvillians aren't known for their sense of style, so don't worry about what to wear when going out- Just be comfortable!

## 4. Where to Stay

Jacksonville is a massive city, so figuring out where to stay can be difficult. After reading this book, you may have a better idea of if you are more interested in spending the bulk of your time at The Beaches or Downtown/ Riverside. These two areas are the most popular places in Jacksonville, but are a good 45 minute drive from each other, so it's best to pick one or the other for your accommodations.

Avoid staying in the middle of Jacksonville, for example off of Southside or JTB (J Turner Butler) Blvd. Although they seem like central locations from the map, they are not walkable, so you will spend all of your time driving from one place to the other.

On the contrary, if you stay in Riverside or The Beaches, you will have many options of activities, sites, and restaurants that are within walking distance.

## 5. How to Get Around

Like most cities in Florida, it is absolutely essential to have a car for your trip to Jacksonville. Jacksonville has been voted as one of the most deadliest cities for pedestrians in the US because there simply aren't sidewalks or bike paths in most areas.

Jacksonville has two main roads to get you from one side of town to the other. I-95 takes you North to South and JTB takes you East to West. Most of Jacksonville is in a giant grid with Downtown and Riverside to the West and The Beaches to the East.

The two areas of town you should stay away from are North Side and West Side. These are very poor areas that have extremely high crime rates, but thankfully, there is really no reason to go near there during your visit.

## 6. Learn the Neighborhoods

In Jacksonville, it's all about the neighborhoods. When you ask someone where they live or where a restaurant is, they will probably respond by saying something like "Riverside" or "The Beaches". This can be confusing for people that don't live in the area, so here are a few of the neighborhood basics:

- **The Beaches**: Refers to anywhere on the coast. The beaches include Jacksonville Beach, Neptune Beach, Atlantic Beach, and Ponte Vedra Beach. More on these later.
- **Riverside:** The hipster part of town located on the St. John River near downtown.
- **San Marco**: Riverside's more mature sibling. Located right across the St. Johns River from Downtown and Riverside.
- **Southside**: Suburban and commercial area of town located around Southside Ave.
- **North Side/ West Side**: Dangerous area- Don't go here.

# 7. Know the Lingo

Jacksonvillians have some unique words. In case you overhear some locals talking, here is a condensed excerpt from the Jacksonville Urban Dictionary:

**Cross the Ditch:** When you have to cross the St. Johns River to get from one side of town to the other. .

**Cruiser:** A type of bicycle with one gear and usually a basket at the front.

**"Duvaaaaallll":** Refers to Duval County. Often yelled by rowdy locals to show support for the city.

**Fixie:** Fixed gear bicycle, most often seen around the Riverside and San Marco neighborhoods.

**Jags:** The Jacksonville Jaguars, Jax's NFL football team.

**Riverside Rat:** A local to the Riverside area.

**PV:** Short for Ponte Vedra

## 8. The Beaches- Which One is Right for You?

Jacksonville is home to 22 miles of sandy white beaches. Known to locals collectively as "The Beaches", they are actually broken up into four distinct areas.

Depending on what you are into, one beach is going to be more appealing to you than the others. Check out each beach description next to see which one is right for you!

## 9. The Beaches: Ponte Vedra Beach

Ponte Vedra Beach, also known as PVB, is home to mansions, exclusive golf clubs, wealthy retirees, and desperate housewives. Unless you have an invitation to the Ponte Vedra Inn & Club, or if you have a friend living in the area, this isn't the best spot for out-of-towners. Most of the beach access points are private and there are no places to park without getting towed.

If you do find yourself in the area though, check out Palm Valley Fish Camp or Barbara Jean's for some delicious grub.

## 10. The Beaches: Jacksonville Beach

Jacksonville Beach, also known as Jax beach, is the most touristy area on the coast. This is where the pier is located, as well as the main shopping area where you can find cheap bathing suits and surfing gear. There are a few beach front restaurants here, but many are overpriced and lack quality. My suggestion is to park in one of the large public parking lots in Jax beach, rent a bike, and head north to Atlantic or Neptune.

On your way here, don't miss Sun Deli. It's a local favorite to grab a sub on your way to la playa.

## 11. The Beaches: Neptune Beach

Neptune Beach is nestled between Jacksonville Beach and Atlantic Beach. This little area has a laid back vibe and is very residential. You won't find any tourists here, and if you can find a place to park, it's the perfect spot for some quiet relaxation. You can also find several restaurants, coffee shops, and boutiques in the area.

## 12. The Beaches: Atlantic Beach

Atlantic Beach is my all-time favorite spot. With a mix of amazing restaurants, bars, and beaches, Atlantic Beach gives you an authentic feeling. You won't find a Longhorn Steakhouse or Cheesecake Factory around, just local and independent goodness.

Some Atlantic Beach favorites are Flying Iguana for amazing cocktails and Mexican food, Ragtime for libations and live music, and North Beach Fish Camp for a classy seafood dinner. If you are in the area during summertime, don't miss Lemon Bar for a crowded, but memorable, Happy Hour right in the sand.

At any time of the year, check out Poe's Tavern for arguably one of the best burgers in the city that also features an amazing local beer selection in the bottle and on tap.

## 13. The Beaches: Talbot Islands

Little Talbot Island and Big Talbot Island are the perfect place for a day trip escape. To get here, either drive on N I-95 and cut over on Hecksher Drive. Or for a more memorable ride, take your car on the ferry from Mayport.

The Talbot Islands are known for their amazing beaches, estuaries, state parks, and kayaking. The best place for some water activities is to make your way over to Kayak Amelia and rent a double or single kayak for the day. Make sure to bring a cooler with food and drinks so you can make a stop along one of the sandy beaches for a picnic during your time on the water.

## 14. The Beaches: Get a Beach Cruiser

No trip to the beach is complete without riding a beach cruiser around the streets, stopping at the local bars and restaurants along the way. There are a number of spots to rent a bike for the day, just don't forget to lock them up when you stop, as unattended bikes have a history of "walking away".

The Beaches are relatively close to each other, so if you can't decide on one beach, spend the day biking up 1st street where you can visit all four.

Keep in mind that biking under the influence is a criminal offense, so drink and bike responsibly.

## 15. The Beaches: St. Augustine

Okay, so St. Augustine isn't technically a part of Jacksonville proper, but it is a go-to spot for Jacksonville locals, so I thought I should tell you about it here.

St. Augustine is famous for being the oldest city in the United States and it has been said that this is where Christopher Columbus first landed. With its beautiful historic Spanish colonial architecture, pristine beaches, and cute boutiques and shops, St. Augustine is a common day trip or weekend trip for locals who want to get out of Jacksonville.

Jessica French

*"At the Beach, life if different. Time doesn't move hour to hour but mood to moment. We live by the currents, plan by the tides, and follow the sun."*

*– Anonymous*

Jessica French

## 16. San Pablo, Hodges & Kernan

When looking at a map of Jacksonville, San Pablo Road, Hodges Blvd, and Kernan Blvd are centrally located and might seem like an idea place to stay- Don't make this mistake.

The only things of interest around here is the University of North Florida and Mayo Hospital, neither of which should be included in your trip (unless you are visiting Jacksonville for medical treatments or to go back to college). This area of town is very residential and you won't find much other than houses, Starbucks, and Publix.

## 17. Business Districts

Not many people know this, but Jacksonville is one of the top cities in Florida for business. Over the years, many well-known companies have relocated their corporate headquarters here from places like New York and San Francisco, because with the cost of living difference, you can employ two people in Jacksonville for the price of one elsewhere.

Some of the most notable employers are Johnson & Johnson, Fidelity National Financial, Bank of America, Baptist Health, and Florida Blue.

All of these businesses are located in two main business districts, one located in Downtown and one located in the Southside area. Other than corporate complexes, these areas have a few unique things to offer as well.

## 18. Business Districts: Southside Restaurants

One of the largest business areas is located near Southside Blvd. Home to companies like Florida Blue and Johnson & Johnson, traffic can get quite crazy during rush hour.

Other than a 9-to-5, you can find a good quality mall, as well as some delicious ethnic food in the area.

My favorites are Nile Ethiopian Restaurant, Pattaya Thai Restaurant, and La Nopalera Mexican Restaurant (known to locals as "La Nop"). Each of these places are worth a visit to Southside on its own.

## 19. Business Districts: The Avenues

Located near many business offices on Southside and Phillips, you can find one of the only two decent shopping malls in the Jacksonville area, The Avenues. The Avenues is an indoor shopping mall that is complete with a movie theater and Cheesecake Factory. Although most locals don't spend much time here, this is one of the only options if you need to make a quick stop by a JC Penny or H&M.

## 20. Business Districts: St. Johns Town Center

Located right next to the complexes of Florida Blue and Johnson & Johnson, you can find an upscale open-air mall, the St. Johns Town Center. Home to all of the normal mall restaurants like Panera, and Maggiano's, you can also find high-end retailers like Chanel, Gucci, and Brooks Brothers.

This is also one of the only places in Jacksonville to find big-box stores like Best Buy, Costco, or BJs. Many employees from the nearby corporate offices visit this complexes for work lunches during the week.

The only restaurant in the complex that is worth going out of your way to visit is Moxie Kitchen & Cocktail. They have amazing food and drinks in a newly built industrial, yet chic building.

Be careful though, parking in the St. Johns Town Center is a nightmare!

## 21. Business Districts: Downtown

What was once a struggling business district, turned ghost town at night, is now going through a major revitalization thanks to organizations including The Elbow and Friends of Hemming Park.

Although The Landing, a once thriving waterfront restaurant and shopping complex, still needs some major work, the pedestrian walkway directly in front of it along the water is something that is not to be missed.

Some Downtown local favorites include 1904 for live music, Dos Gatos for cocktails in a speakeasy setting, and the beautiful Museum of Modern Art (MoMA).

## 22. Riverside: Hang with the Hipsters

Grab a flannel shirt, throw on your skinny jeans, and hop on your fixie- We are heading to Riverside! Located right on the side of the St. Johns River, and next to Downtown, Riverside has all of the local coffee shops, microbreweries, vegan restaurants, and farm-to-table goodness that you could ever dream of. This is where the alternative and artsy crew hangs out and they know how to have a good time.

The Beaches and Riverside have always had a rivalry. People that live in one rarely ever venture over to the other. It's the clash of the bud light and beach bros versus the quinoa and craft cocktail kids. I don't know about you, but I'm siding with the latter.

Jessica French

*"There's nothing more dangerous than someone who wants to make the world a better place" - Banksy*

Jessica French

## 23. Riverside: Sun Ray Cinema

One of Riverside's most iconic venues is Sun Ray Cinema. Sun Ray is a tiny two theater cinema where you can watch independent films, in addition to some big new releases, while eating vegan pizza and drinking local craft beer all for half the price of your big-box AMC.

Popular for date nights, a night out with friends, or a solo Saturday afternoon, Sun Ray is one of the most amazing independent businesses that exists in the area today.

On top of the fact that you can eat and drink while watching a movie, they have an epic popcorn bar with toppings like curry powder, siracha, truffle oil, and old bay spice. With so many choices, you will keep coming back for more!

## 24. Riverside: Restaurants

Hipsters love a good farm-to-table meal and cocktail, so the Riverside area has no shortage of food and drink purveyors. I have listed a few of my favorites below:

**Hawkers:** Asian tapas and sharable plates

**Ale Wife:** Craft beers and board games

**Birdies:** Late night dancing

**Rain Dogs:** Beer and wine only dive bar

**BREW:** Coffee shop with delicious toasts and baked goods

**Corner Taco:** Tacos and Mexican fare with vegan options

**Grassroots:** Natural market with juices and smoothies

**Black Sheep:** Rooftop brunch spot

**Orsay:** French-fusion with a killer happy hour

**Sumo Sushi:** Small but high-quality sushi spot

## 25. Riverside: Parks

Riverside is home to some of the city's best parks. On the weekends, you can frequently find locals hanging out on the grassy lawns, enjoying a picnic under the shade of the pine trees. Some of the best parks are Memorial Park, Riverside Park, and Willowbranch Park.

Grab a blanket and a book and get ready to enjoy Florida's year-round beautiful weather.

## 26. Riverside: The St. John's River

One of Jacksonville's natural beauties is the St. John's River that flows through the entire city. The St. Johns is a dividing landmark that separates Riverside and Downtown from San Marco, Southside, and The Beaches.

Unfortunately, due to pollution, you definitely don't want to go for a swim in this majestic river, but it's perfect for other water activities. If you can find a boat, fishing is extremely popular on the St. Johns, as well as kayaking in one of its smaller estuaries.

## 27. Cultural Activities

Due to its sunny year round weather, Jacksonville hosts many cultural events and activities. From arts markets to music festivals, and from food festivals to holiday spectaculars, there will most likely be a few events going on while you come to visit. For the latest activities, visit Facebook or check our Jacksonville, Florida events on Google.

## 28. Cultural Activities: Jacksonville Art Walk

Art Walk is a lively event that is hosted in Downtown Jacksonville on the first Wednesday of every month from 5pm-9pm. During this time, the streets are blocked off and are bustling with local vendors, artists, activities, and musicians. You can grab some food from a food truck, pop in an art gallery, or peruse the Museum of Modern Art (MoMA) which is free during Art Walk. Even though the official festivities end at 9pm, if you don't want the fun to stop, the local bars at the Elbow usually have some after party activities.

## 29. Cultural Activities: Riverside Arts Market

Every Saturday from 10am-4pm, the Riverside Arts Market (RAM) can be found bustling with locals and tourists alike under the I-95 bridge. Each week's market has a theme, including my personal favorites Yoga Market and Arf Barket.

The usual vendors range from hand crafted clothes and jewelry to homemade soaps, pickles, and soups. There is also a Farmers Row featuring locally grown fruits, vegetables, and honey. This is where many locals get their veggies for the week!

RAM is always complete with a free 9am yoga class before the market kicks off and then features local actors, singers, and performers on the main stage throughout the day's festivities.

# 30. Cultural Activities: The PLAYERS Championship

Every year, on the week of Mother's Day, Jacksonville hosts one of the most lively golf events in the nation, the PGA Tour's The PLAYERS Championship, also known as TPC. Even if you are not a golf fan, this is a must see event.

Hosted on one of the most prestigious golf courses in the country, Sawgrass Stadium Course, TPC is a week of mingling, eating, and exploring with Jacksonville's finest.

This all day event that starts early in the morning where you can find patrons congregating at one of the many bloody mary or mimosa bars. If you can afford it, definitely go for an upgraded ticket that includes access to one of the tents. It gets very hot and tiring walking around in the sun all day and being able to retreat into an air conditioned tent is oh so worth it.

## 31. Cultural Activities: Jacksonville Jazz Fest

Every year in May, typically coinciding with Memorial Day, Downtown Jacksonville shuts down to host the Jacksonville Jazz Festival. The festival lasts for three days and has been dubbed by experts as one of the top jazz festivals in the nation.

Past performers have included Miles Davis, Dizzy Gillespie, George Benson, Dianne Reeves, and Chris Botti.

## 32. Cultural Activities: Florida-Georgia

Known as 'The World's Largest Outdoor Cocktail Party', every year in Jacksonville, two of the largest football rivals face off, The Florida Gators and the University of Georgia Bulldogs. The first game was played in 1904 and has been played every season since 1926, except for a war-time interruption in 1943.

During this week, fans and football enthusiasts alike flock to downtown Jacksonville, which essentially shuts down for the duration of the game day activities.

## 33. Cultural Activities: Gate River Run

The Gate River Run is an annual 15k hosted in Jacksonville that has been ongoing since the first road race in 1994. The event is always complete with vendors, live music, and a large party at the finish line and is the premier racing event for any serious runner in the area. Every year, over 15,000 runners participate in the Gate River Run and they have recently added a 1-mile and 5k run/walk for charity.

## 34. Cultural Activities: One Spark

Started in 2013, One Spark is a relatively new event that was started to showcase and support the new startup culture in Jacksonville. Every year, creators sign up and showcase their inventions and creations that are separated into art, innovation, music, science, technology, and social good categories.

During the three day event, attendees can vote for their favorite creators who then face off in a "shark tank" like showdown for a chance to win cash prizes.

In addition to the creator competition, One Spark also showcases local music, activities, food, and drink.

## 35. Cultural Activities: 4<sup>th</sup> of July Fireworks

In regards to holidays, the 4th of July celebration is what Jacksonville is best known for. Travelers from Georgia and the surrounding Florida areas come to Jacksonville Beach for the fireworks display and to enjoy a fun day in the sun.

In addition to the fireworks display at the Jacksonville pier, Downtown Jacksonville usually puts on a firework display which thousands watch from the waterfront The Landings Complex.

## 36. Cultural Activities: Brew at the Zoo

Every year, the Jacksonville Zoo & Gardens hosts their always sold-out event, Brew at the Zoo. During Brew at the Zoo, food and drink vendors from around Jacksonville are featured, games and activities are played, and the entire zoo is open for guests to visit.

All profits from the event go to supporting the zoo to help them care for their 2,000 animals and over 1,000 plants.

## 37. Sports

Jacksonville is home to a number of professional sports teams. As with many Florida cities, sports are a big part of Jacksonville and the area seems to shut down when there is a big game in town.

Aside from professional sports, Jacksonville locals can often be found playing on kickball teams or playing beach volleyball in their free time.

## 38. Sports- The Jacksonville Jaguars

The Jacksonville Jaguars, known locally as the Jags, is Jacksonville's National Football League (NFL) team. The Jags play at EverBank Field, located Downtown, and the owner of the team, Shahid Khan, is Jacksonville's mustached legend (more on this later).

Although the Jags haven't been very good at playing football in a while, Shahid Khan helped finance a $63 million improvement to EverBank Field which started in November of 2013. These new improvements include two 362 ft scoreboards which are the largest HD LED boards in the world, two infinity wading pools with cabanas looking over each end zone, and top of the line club seating and walkout patios. Although the football playing hasn't gotten much better, locals flock to these games now, more or less, to enjoy the new stadium.

# 39. Sports- The Jacksonville Jumbo Shrimp

Formerly known as the Jacksonville Suns, The Jacksonville Jumbo Shrimp are Jacksonville's Minor League Baseball team. The Jumbo Shrimp play at the Baseball Grounds of Jacksonville, also located Downtown, but they draw a much smaller crown than the Jags.

Known most for their Thirsty Thursday promotions, locals typically go to the games because of the cheap tickets and dollar beers.

In November of 2016, the team changed their name from the Jacksonville Suns to the Jacksonville Jumbo Shrimp, which upset many Jacksonvillians. The team has also been known for other odd antics like distributing free pregnancy tests at their "You Might Be a Father's Day" game promotion.

## 40. Sports- The Jacksonville IceMen & More

Other than the Jacksonville Jags and the Jacksonville Jumbo Shrimp, Jacksonville is home to a few other notable sports teams as well.

The Jacksonville IceMen is the local ice hockey team.

The Jacksonville Sharks is the local indoor football team.

The Jacksonville Axemen is a local rugby team.

The Jacksonville Giants is the local basketball team

Outside of professional sports, Jacksonville's two universities, Jacksonville University (JU) and the University of North Florida (UNF), have been known to have notable athletics departments as well.

*"A Bad Day in Florida is Still Better than A Good Day*

*Anywhere Else"*

Jessica French

## 41. Notable Places- Florida Theater

The Florida Theater is located in Downtown Jacksonville and was opened in 1927. Now on the US National Register of Historic Places, The Florida Theater used to be one of the most notable movie theaters of its time, particularly during the Golden Age of Hollywood.

After it's closing in 1980, the Florida Theater was purchased by the Arts Assembly of Jacksonville who began an extensive renovation. Today, the Florida theater is home to the Florida Ballet and still boasts the notoriety that Elvis Presley played two shows there in 1956.

## 42. Notable Places- The Jacksonville Landing

The Jacksonville Landing sits on a prime piece of real estate right on the St. Johns River in the heart of Downtown. The 120,000+ square foot facility was opened in 1987 and used to be one of the most happening places in the area, with restaurants, a video arcade, and retail spaces.

Unfortunately, over many years, The Landing slowly declined, restaurants and retailers moved out, and it now sits half abandoned. Although a few tenants still remain, the crowd that frequents The Landing is usually the local derelicts.

A huge discussion in Jacksonville right now is what to do with The Landing, but no serious progress or plans have been made yet.

## 43. Notable Places- St. Augustine Amphitheatre

The St. Augustine Ampitheatre was built in 1965 and is an extremely popular outdoor concert venue, just a few minutes from the historic St. Augustine downtown area. Many Jacksonvillians head to the Ampitheatre for large shows and festivals, which has featured artists including Jack Johnson, Earth Wind and Fire, Lynyrd Skynyrd, and The Avett Brothers.

## 44. Notable Places- Jacksonville Zoo & Gardens

The Jacksonville Zoo and Gardens opened in 1914 and has over 2,000 species of plants and animals. The Zoo is located in North Jacksonville, near the International Airport, and sits at the mouth of the Trout River.

The main areas of the Zoo are the Great Apes of the World, Wild Florida, Australian Adventure, Stingray Bay, and Range of the Jaguar.

## 45. Nature

Jacksonville is home to the largest urban park system in the United States. With over 337 locations, encompassing more than 80,000 acres, one of the beautiful things about Jacksonville is how you can easily get to a nature park or reserve just as easily as you can get to a bustling urban center.

These state and national parks are home to a diverse range of flora and fauna. A trip to Jacksonville would not be complete without visiting one of the beautiful parks in the area.

## 46. Nature- Guana National Wildlife Preserve

If you enjoy hiking, you have to head Guana Tolomato Matanzas National Wildlife Reserve, located just south of Ponte Vedra Beach. With over 15+ miles of unique hiking trails, you will encounter a variety of different ecological areas in one trip including sandy beaches, oyster beds, estuaries, and dense forests. During my trips to Guana, I have encountered tortoises, alligators, racoons, armadillos, white tailed deer, snakes, and birds. Please be respectful of the animals though... They won't bother you if you don't bother them!

Local tip- There is a pristine stretch of beach directly across A1A from the hiking trails which is perfect for a post-hike dip!

## 47. Nature- Amelia Island State Park

Amelia Island State Park is located just seven miles north of Little Talbot Island State Park, just off of A1A. The park consists of 200 acres of salt marshes, forests, and beaches. Some of the most common activities you can do in the park include fishing, hiking, and horseback riding.

Amelia Island State park also has some of the most pristine beaches in the area and is a popular place for locals to go to search for sharks teeth.

During the summer time, you can also come to Amelia Island to watch female turtles lay their eggs and then come back later in the season to watch them hatch.

## 48. Nature- Fort Clinch State Park

Fort Clinch State Park is home to over 1,400 acres of hiking, beaches, and wildlife areas. You can also tour around the remains of an old fort that was used during the Civil War and see soldiers reenact the skills they used to use such as carpentry, blacksmithing, and masonry.

Hiking at Fort Clinch State Park is another way to spend the day, during which you will most likely encounter deer, turtles, snakes, and the occasional alligator.

## 49. Nature- Anastasia State Park

Anastasia State Park is located near downtown St. Augustine and is also home to the St. Augustine Ampitheater. The park is home to many plants and animals in a tidal salt marsh setting.

Aside from coming to the Amphitheater to watch live music, visitors to the park often go swimming, surfing, and kayaking.

## 50. The Legend- Shahid Khan

No book about Jacksonville would be complete without a word about its unofficial mayor, Shahid Khan. Also knows as Shad Khan, Shad came to America from Pakistan at the age of 16 with just a couple of dollars in his pocket. After graduating from college, Shad started working at a manufacturing company which he later took a loan out from the SBA to purchase the company from his former employer.

Shad is now a business tycoon who has been featured on the cover of Forbes magazine and is ranked as the 70th richest American, and 158th richest person in the world, with a net worth of over $8.7 billion.

In 2011, Shad purchased Jacksonville's NFL team, the Jacksonville Jaguars, and is known for funding the major renovation to the EverBank stadium in 2013.

## Top Reasons to Book This Trip

- Beaches: With four beaches in total and year-round sunny weather, you can spend an entire vacation at The Beaches having fun in the sun.

- Nature: Home to the largest urban park system in the nation, Jacksonville has endless local, state, and national parks.

- Fair Price: Jacksonville is an extremely cheap place to visit compared with other Florida locations, like Orlando or Miami.

Jessica French

# > TOURIST

## GREATER THAN A TOURIST

Visit GreaterThanATourist.com
http://GreaterThanATourist.com

Sign up for the Greater Than a Tourist Newsletter
http://eepurl.com/cxspyf

Follow us on Facebook:
https://www.facebook.com/GreaterThanATourist

Follow us on Pinterest:
http://pinterest.com/GreaterThanATourist

Follow us on Instagram:
http://Instagram.com/GreaterThanATourist

Jessica French

# > TOURIST

## GREATER THAN A TOURIST

Please leave your honest review of this book on Amazon and Goodreads.  Thank you.

We appreciate your positive and negative feedback as we try to provide  tourist guidance  in their next trip from a local.

## Our Story

Traveling is a passion of the "Greater than a Tourist" series creator. Lisa studied abroad in college, and for their honeymoon Lisa and her husband toured Europe. During her travels to Malta, an older man tried to give her some advice based on his own experience living on the island since he was a young boy. She was not sure if she should talk to the stranger but was interested in his advice. When traveling to some places she was wary to talk to locals because she was afraid that they weren't being genuine. Through her travels, Lisa learned how much locals had to share with tourists. Lisa created the "Greater Than a Tourist" book series to help connect people with locals. A topic that locals are very passionate about sharing.

Jessica French

Notes

Made in the USA
Monee, IL
23 June 2023

36827653R00052